Adventures
in the Air

SIMON LEWIS

A+
Smart Apple Media

Smart Apple Media is published by Black Rabbit Books
P.O. Box 3263, Mankato, Minnesota 56002

Printed in Hong Kong

Library of Congress Cataloging-in-Publication Data

Lewis, Simon.
    Adventures in the air / Simon Lewis.
    p. cm.—(Smart Apple Media. Difficult & dangerous)
    Summary: The true stories of Manfred von Richthofen (the Red Baron), Charles Lindbergh, Amelia Earhart, Chuck Yeager, and Steve Fossett, who all broke records in flight—Provided by publisher.
Includes index.
    ISBN 978-1-59920-161-0
    1. Air pilots—Biography—Juvenile literature. 2. Aeronautics—Records—Juvenile literature. I. Title.
TL539.L46 2009
629.13092'2—dc22

                                                                                                2008000431

All words in **bold** can be found in the glossary on pages 30–31.

Web site information is correct at time of going to press. However, the publishers cannot accept liability for any information or links found on third-party Web sites.

Created by Q2AMedia
Series Editor: Jean Coppendale
Book Editor: Corrine Ochiltree
Senior Art Designers: Ashita Murgai, Nishant Mudgal
Designer: Shilpi Sarkar
Picture Researcher: Lalit Dalal
Line Artists: Amit Tayal, Sibi N.D
Illustrators: Mahender Kumar, Sanyogita Lal

Picture credits
t=top b=bottom c=center l=left r=right m=middle
Cover: Q2AMedia
Bettmann/ Corbis: 4, Sheila Terry/ SPL/ Photolibrary: 5t, Richard Cooke/ Alamy: 5b, PPL Ltd/ Rex Features: 6t, A Henry/ AWM: 9, Lindbergh Picture Collection. Manuscripts & Archives, Yale University Library: 11, The Print Collector/ Alamy: 15, Corbis: 16t, Popperfoto/ Alamy: 19t, Bettmann/ Corbis: 20t, Purdue University Libraries, Archives and Special Collections: 20b, AF.MIL: 21, JPL/ NASA: 23l, 23r, AF.MIL: 25, Virgin Atlantic Global Flyer: 26, 27tb, 28

Contents

REACHING FOR THE SKIES

From earliest times, people have dreamed of conquering the skies. Today, traveling by plane is no more difficult or dangerous than going by train or car. But it was not always so. The history of aviation is full of men and women who risked their lives in order to fly higher, faster, and farther than human beings had ever flown before.

The First Aviators

In early times, people tried to fly like birds by attaching wings to their arms. It was not until 1903, when the Wright brothers combined cleverly crafted wings on a wooden frame with a lightweight gasoline engine, that the world's first powered airplane, the *Kitty Hawk*, took to the skies. On December 17, the brothers made three flights, the longest lasting 59 seconds. Six years later, French pilot Louis Blériot flew across the English Channel for the first time.

*The Wright brothers, Orville and Wilbur, were the first to achieve a successful flight in a heavier-than-air **fixed-wing** aircraft.*

4

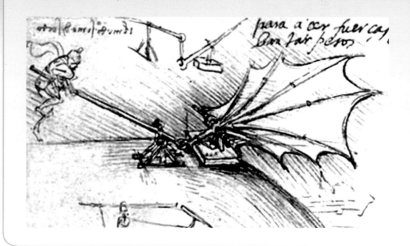

In early times, people tried to fly by imitating the flapping motion of a bird's wings. This sketch by the artist and inventor Leonardo da Vinci was made in about 1488. It shows an artificial wing being moved rapidly up and down by means of a lever.

Flying Fighters

The first main use of airplanes was in warfare. In World War I, the German flying ace Baron von Richthofen (see page 6) showed how deadly fighter planes could be. Later, pilots such as Charles Lindbergh and Amelia Earhart used their skills and courage to make ever longer and more dangerous flights. Bigger and better planes were being built all the time. Even today, aviators are testing human endurance and technology to the limits.

Displays by skilled aerobatics teams such as the British Red Arrows show the speed and agility of modern fighter planes.

THE RED BARON

Manfred von Richthofen

The German Baron Manfred von Richthofen (1891–1918) was the most successful fighter pilot of World War I. He became known as the "Red Baron" because he flew a bright red Fokker **triplane**. In only 20 months, Richthofen shot down 80 Allied aircraft. The sight of Richthofen's red plane was enough to strike terror in the hearts of Allied fighter pilots.

One of the most highly skilled and feared of all flying **aces**, the Red Baron received 24 military **decorations** for his services.

GREAT BRITAIN

London

Cambrai

GERMANY

BELGIUM

Paris

FRANCE

Western Front

Map of the Western Front in 1916 shows Cambrai in Occupied France, where the Red Baron scored his first victory.

The First Kill

Richthofen began his career with the German air force in the early days of World War I. After only 21 hours of training, he made his first solo flight—and crash-landed! But soon his flying exploits so impressed his superiors that he was chosen to fly with the Germans' top unit, Jagdstaffel 2. On September 1, 1916, Richthofen reported for duty on the Western Front. Soon after, he shot down his first enemy plane over Cambrai, France.

> " . . . He knew exactly that his last hour had arrived at the moment when I got at the back of him. At that time I had not yet the conviction 'He must fall!' which I have now on such occasions . . ."
>
> Baron von Richthofen describing his first kill in his autobiography, *The Red Battle Flyer (1917)*

The Red Baron closes in on his prey during a fierce **dogfight** over the Western Front.

Richthofen leads his unit, Jagdgeschwader 1, on a combat mission. The unit was nick-named the "Flying Circus" because of the bright colors of the planes and the large circus-like tents where the pilots and their machines were housed.

Circus of Death

By January 1917, Richthofen had destroyed 16 enemy planes and was a national hero. The German **High Command** even tried to prevent him from flying in order to protect him from injury. But nothing could keep the Red Baron away from the action. On April 29, he shot down four planes in one day—a personal best—and reached an all-time record of 41 enemy planes shot down in total.

The Baron's Last Flight

In July 1917, Richthofen was shot down by an English plane. Despite a bullet wound to the head, he survived and was soon back in the air. On September 1, he shot down his sixtieth plane. Then, on April 21, 1918, the Red Baron began his last, fatal flight. During a fierce dogfight, a Canadian pilot dived on the Baron's bloodred Fokker from above, while Australian ground soldiers fired from below. Richthofen's plane was hit. The Australians recovered the plane and the body of the greatest combat pilot ever known. The reign of the Red Baron was over.

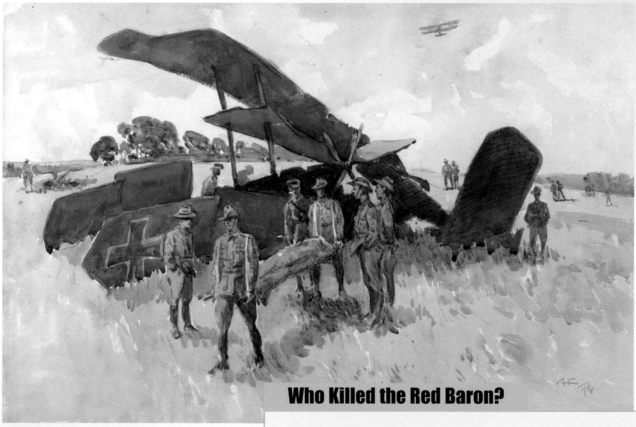

A postcard of the time shows Australian servicemen removing the body of the Red Baron from the wreckage of his Fokker triplane.

Who Killed the Red Baron?

Richthofen died of a bullet wound to the chest. Various individuals claimed the honor of bringing him down, but no one knows for certain who fired the fatal shot.

Richthofen was buried in France with full military honors. Germany went into deep mourning at the loss of their hero. In 1925, his body was returned to Germany and given the largest funeral ever seen in Berlin.

Master of the Skies

Before joining the air force, Richthofen had been an eager hunter and had learned skills that were vital for aerial combat. As a pilot, he loved the thrill of the chase, was a quick thinker, stuck to his target, and fired fast. He was also a master of tactics such as diving "out of the sun" or swooping under an enemy plane to fire at it from below.

German pilots had no parachutes; it was thought to encourage cowardice if they could ditch their planes to get out of trouble!

The German Fokker planes were fast and agile. But they had one big drawback: the Lewis gun mounted on the fuselage could only be fired forward or upward—it did not swivel around like the guns of the British Sopwith Camels. This left the pilot very exposed.

How Would YOU Survive?

1 Which of these qualities would you need to survive an encounter with the deadly Red Baron?

Nerves of steel	Ruthlessness	Decisiveness
Sharp eyes	Calmness	Fear of heights
Team spirit	Honesty	Lightning reflexes
Friendliness	Easy-going nature	Reckless courage

2 If you had a choice, which plane would you rather fly, a Fokker or a Sopwith Camel?

Fokker	Sopwith Camel
Guns could only fire upward or forward	*Guns could turn from side to side*
Could climb quickly	*Faster than the Fokker*
Easy to control	*Could easily spin out of control*

A PASSION FOR PLANES
Charles Lindbergh's Solo Transatlantic Flight

Born in Detroit in 1902, Charles Lindbergh always had a passion for planes. As a young man, he trained as a pilot, bought a plane of his own, and even took a job as a stunt flyer.

While working as an airmail delivery pilot, Lindbergh heard of a prize of $25,000 being offered for the first person to fly nonstop from New York to Paris. Nothing like this had ever been attempted. It was a challenge an adventurer such as Lindbergh could not resist.

The Journey of a Lifetime

Deciding to fly single-handed in order to carry more fuel, Lindbergh planned the flight to the last detail. By April 28, 1927, his plane, the *Spirit of St. Louis*, had been designed and built to meet his exact requirements. After short test flights, he set out from San Diego to Long Island, a distance nearly equal to that from New York to Paris. He made it in 21 hours 20 minutes, setting a new coast-to-coast record. He was ready to begin the journey of his life.

Once dubbed "the flying fool" because of his reckless courage, Charles Lindbergh (1902–74) is recognized today as one of the great pioneers of aviation.

Alone in the Mid-Atlantic

On the morning of May 20, 1927, a crowd of 500 gathered to watch the *Spirit of St. Louis* take off from Roosevelt Field on Long Island. Spectators gasped as the plane, holding 450 gallons (1,700 L) of fuel, narrowly missed the **telegraph** wires and trees at the end of the dirt runway. Moments later, Lindbergh had set course and was heading safely for the Atlantic.

Storm Ahead!

By the time Lindbergh reached Newfoundland, night was falling and storm clouds were gathering. Thick fog surrounded the plane, hiding the ocean from view. Fearing that ice would form on the cockpit and wings, Lindbergh struggled to avoid the storm and still stay on course. Tiredness was setting in. Despite the freezing cold, he opened the cockpit windows to keep himself awake.

Lashed by wind and freezing sleet, Lindbergh battled the Atlantic storm clouds. Even today, ice is a deadly hazard for planes, limiting visibility, adding weight, and reducing the flow of air over the wings.

"The tops of the storm clouds were several thousand feet above me and at one time, when I attempted to fly through one of the larger clouds, sleet started to collect on the plane. I was forced to turn around and get back into clear air immediately."

Charles Lindbergh,
The Spirit of St. Louis (1953)

Saturday, May 21, 1927

By dawn the next morning, Lindbergh was once more enveloped in a thick bank of fog. The hours that followed were among the most difficult and dangerous of the flight. By 7:52 A.M., he had been airborne for 24 hours and was struggling to keep exhaustion at bay. Time and again he thought he could see shorelines in the distance and trees outlined against the horizon. He later wrote: "The **mirages** were so natural that, had I not been in mid-Atlantic and known that no land existed along my route, I would have taken them to be actual islands."

Lindbergh: The Facts

3,610 miles (5,810 km)

USA
Newfoundland
NORTH ATLANTIC
New York

GREAT BRITAIN
IRELAND
Paris
FRANCE
SPAIN

THE ROUTE

On paper, Lindbergh's route looks curved. In fact, his flight plan took advantage of the curve in the earth's surface to give him the shortest possible distance between New York and Paris.

THE PLANE

Inside the *Spirit of St. Louis*, the cockpit was so small that Lindbergh could not even stretch his legs. His only view was out of the side windows and via a **periscope** mounted on the left side of the plane.

With so much space taken up by fuel tanks, Lindbergh only had room for the bare essentials.

LINDBERGH'S EQUIPMENT LIST

2 flashlights	2 canteens
1 ball of string	1 cup
1 ball of cord	1 air raft with pump
1 hunting knife	
4 red flares	5 cans army rations
1 box of matches	2 air cushions
1 large needle	1 hacksaw blade

"Which Way to Ireland?"

By morning, the skies had cleared. Lindbergh was over halfway to Paris. The bright sunshine revived him briefly, but soon tiredness overcame him again. He even fell asleep at the controls, but only for a moment.

At around 3 P.M., he saw fishing boats below. He circled low, yelling "Which way to Ireland?" but got no reply. Soon he saw the coast of Ireland and set course for France. By 10 P.M., he was flying over Paris. He circled the **Eiffel Tower**, then flew straight to the field at Le Bourget where he landed at 11:22 P.M. It had taken him 33 hours, 30 minutes, and 29.5 seconds to travel nonstop from New York to Paris. He had done it!

> *"It is the greatest shot of **adrenaline** to be doing what you have wanted to do so badly. You almost feel like you could fly without the plane."*
>
> Charles Lindbergh

Hero's Welcome

Lindbergh was an instant hero on both sides of the Atlantic. On his return to New York, thousands lined the streets to welcome him back. His epic flight had put aviation on the map. From then on, people began to take a greater interest in planes and what they could do.

When he saw fishing boats below, Lindbergh knew his goal was within reach. Less than an hour later, the southwest coast of Ireland came into view.

Could YOU Fly Solo Across the Atlantic?

Have you got what it takes to fly across the Atlantic alone and without sleep for over 33 hours? Choose a, b, or c from the questions below and then check your score.

a) My favorite vacation is camping with lots of friends.
b) I like going to museums and galleries.
c) I like to go to the beach with my best friends.

a) I love parties!
b) I like to read or listen to music.
c) I enjoy chatting with friends.

a) My favorite subject is phy. ed.
b) My favorite subject is science.
c) My favorite subject is English.

a) I get easily bored.
b) I can always think of something to do.
c) I like activities with lots of other people.

Score:

Mostly As: You are active and like to be outdoors with lots of people. Spending time by yourself in a small plane would not be much fun for you.

Mostly Bs: You do not mind being alone and could find ways to keep yourself amused during a long, lonely flight at night.

Mostly Cs: You are one of the gang and enjoy being part of a team—perhaps you should stay on the ground!

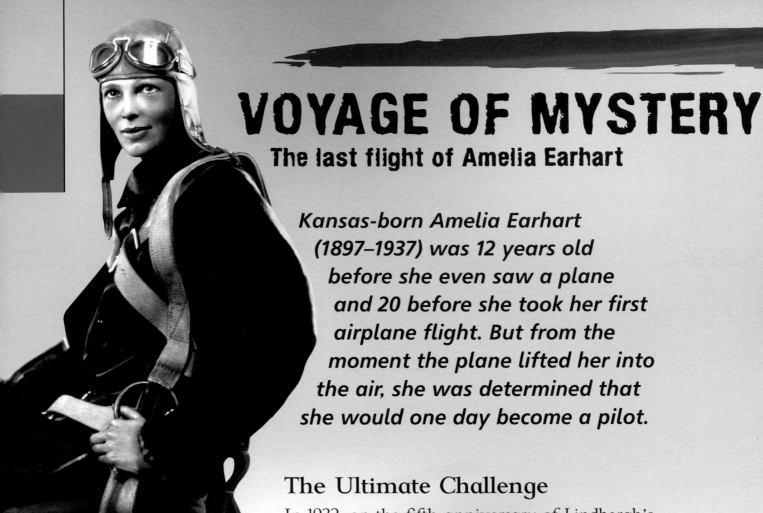

VOYAGE OF MYSTERY
The last flight of Amelia Earhart

Kansas-born Amelia Earhart (1897–1937) was 12 years old before she even saw a plane and 20 before she took her first airplane flight. But from the moment the plane lifted her into the air, she was determined that she would one day become a pilot.

Amelia Earhart's daring and courage inspired many other women to live their dreams.

The Ultimate Challenge

In 1932, on the fifth anniversary of Lindbergh's transatlantic flight, the young aviator Amelia Earhart stormed into the record books, becoming the first woman—and only the second person—to fly solo across the Atlantic Ocean. Many other outstanding flying achievements followed. But at the age of 40, Earhart's greatest challenge still lay ahead of her: to fly around the world.

Earhart's Lockheed Elektra 10E takes off from Lae, New Guinea, on the final leg of her around-the-world flight.

Epic Flight

Earhart's first attempt at an around-the-world flight was thwarted in March 1937 when a tire of her plane blew at takeoff. Her second attempt began on June 1 when she and **navigator** Fred Noonan successfully took off from Miami in their Lockheed Elektra 10E, bound for South America.

The first leg of Earhart's epic flight took her across South America, Africa, and South-East Asia. At midnight on July 2, she and Fred Noonan took off from Lae in New Guinea for the final and most hazardous part of their journey—a 7,000-m (11,265-km) flight over the Pacific. It was a journey that would end in one of the great mysteries of modern times.

"Not much more than a month ago I was on the other shore of the Pacific, looking westward. This evening, I looked eastward over the Pacific. In the fast-moving days which have intervened, the whole width of the world has passed behind us — except this broad ocean. I shall be glad when we have the hazards of its navigation behind us."

Amelia Earhart, before take-off on the final stage of her flight

Earhart's Flight Plan

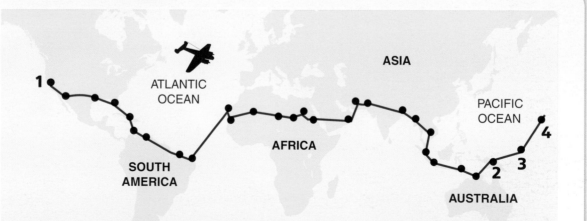

1 May 21, 1937 Leaves Oakland, California.

2 June 29 Arrives in Lae, New Guinea, 22,000 miles (35,400 km) from start.

3 July 2 Leaves Lae for Howland Island. Never arrives.

4 July 4–5 Faint distress signals received from Phoenix Islands.

Lost Without a Trace

Earhart was aiming for Howland Island, a tiny speck in the mid-Pacific, where a U.S. Coast Guard boat, *Itasca*, was waiting to guide her in to land. About 810 miles (1,300 km) into the flight, a crackle over the radio told Earhart that the *Itasca* was in position and standing by. Earhart radioed back to acknowledge the message. Although the crew of the *Itasca* could hear Earhart's voice over the radio, it was clear that the signals Earhart was receiving from the boat were becoming fainter and fainter.

Could Earhart and Noonan have made a forced landing on the nearby Phoenix Islands, south of Howland?

Amelia Earhart at the controls of her plane.

Smoke Signals

Unable to maintain two-way radio contact, the *Itasca* struggled for nearly six hours to guide the plane toward land. At one point, the crew even sent up smoke signals to indicate their position. Finally all contact with the plane was lost. Amelia Earhart, Fred Noonan, and the plane were never seen again.

The Mystery Deepens

For days after Earhart's disappearance, U.S. naval ships combed the area, but nothing was found. On July 4-5, distress calls from the plane were picked up by radio operators across the Pacific, but the signals were not strong enough for its position to be pinpointed. Some think Earhart may have mistaken the shadow of a cloud on the water for land and ditched the plane into the sea. Others believe she was captured by the Japanese and held as an American spy. Many have claimed to have found wreckage of the plane, but nothing conclusive has ever been proved. Perhaps we will never know what really happened.

What Went Wrong?

Why did Earhart fail to land on Howland Island? No one knows, but possible reasons are:

- Neither Earhart nor Noonan were experienced in **radio navigation.**
- The plane and the boat were using **time systems** that were half an hour apart.
- Part of the plane's radio equipment may have been damaged on take-off from New Guinea.

Amelia Earhart's Legacy

Over the past 80 years, countless books and articles have been written about Amelia Earhart's disappearance, but the riddle is no closer to being solved. One good outcome from the tragedy is that new ways were found to improve radio communication. These are now followed by ships and pilots all over the world.

This is the last known photograph of Amelia Earhart and her navigator Fred Noonan with their Lockheed Elektra 10E.

Can YOU Solve the Mystery?

1 Which theory about Amelia Earhart's disappearance do you think is the most likely? Do some research and make a list of three arguments for and against each theory.

- The plane crashed into the sea and Earhart and Noonan drowned.
- The plane crashed on an island and both survived.
- They were both spies.

2 Which do you think would be the worst place to be lost? Why?

- In a scorching desert.
- In the frozen Antarctic.
- Flying over a snow-capped mountain range.
- In the Amazon rainforest.
- At sea in an open boat.
- In space.

SUPERSONIC HERO

Chuck Yeager and the Flight of the *Bell X-1*

*After World War II, the race was on to develop the fastest fighter plane in the world. The world's great **superpowers** knew that security lay in controlling the skies—and the key to air supremacy was speed.*

In the United States, the flight research agency National Advisory Committee for Aeronautics (NACA) had developed a plane that could fly faster than the speed of sound. The trouble was, no pilot was willing to fly it!

Enter Chuck Yeager

One man would change everything. Born in 1923, Chuck Yeager had earned a reputation during the war as a quick-thinking and fearless fighter pilot. In 1946, he was stationed with the U.S. Air Force at Muroc Airfield, California. With nerves of steel and outstanding flying skills, Yeager was the obvious choice for the supreme challenge in aviation: to test-fly NACA's rocket-powered *Bell X-1*.

What Is the "Sound Barrier"?

Austrian physicist Ernst Mach (1838–1916) first recorded the existence of a "barrier" created by fast-flying objects. As an aircraft approaches the speed of sound, **shockwaves** build up in front of the plane and create a barrier that is difficult to break through. At the same time, a **vapor cloud** is produced around the aircraft, which it appears to fly through.

Chuck Yeager's flying career lasted more than 60 years. He was awarded many medals, including the Distinguished Service Medal, the Purple Heart for Bravery, and the Presidential Medal of Freedom.

The Flying Bullet

Like its predecessor, the British de *Havilland 108*, the design of the *Bell X-1* was based on the shape of a 50-caliber bullet—and to fly it at full speed was highly dangerous. But Chuck Yeager was ready for anything. On an early test flight at Muroc Airfield, shockwaves turned the plane into little more than an unguided missile. Narrowly escaping injury, Yeager managed to land safely and was soon preparing for another attempt.

How Fast Is Supersonic?

The speed of sound, Mach 1, varies according to the temperature of the atmosphere—it will be different over hot land and cool water. The speed of sound at sea level is 761.2 miles per hour (1,225.1 km/h).

Yeager named all his planes Glamorous Glennis, *after his wife. The* Bell X-1 *was painted orange because it was thought it would be easier for the camera and tracker plane to keep sight of it. (In fact, white is a better color for this.)*

Broken Ribs

On October 12, 1947, two nights before the flight, Yeager fell off his horse and broke two ribs. Worried that he might not be allowed to fly, he secretly visited a veterinary surgeon in another town and asked to be bandaged up. On the day of the flight, he was in such pain that another pilot had to help him climb into the cockpit.

The *Bell X-1* was loaded aboard a Boeing 29, taken to a height of 22,965 feet (7,000 m) and launched. The moment had come. Yeager ignited the rocket chambers and kept accelerating until he had blasted through the sound barrier with over 6,000 pounds (2,700 kg) of **thrust**. He kept going and flew faster than the speed of sound for approximately 20 seconds before slowing down and landing. The sound barrier had been broken.

> "I thought I was seeing things! We were flying **supersonic**! And it was as smooth as a baby's bottom: Grandma could be sitting up there sipping lemonade."
>
> Chuck Yeager, on his first supersonic flight

Muroc Airfield (Edwards Air Force Base)

Muroc Airfield, on the edge of California's Mojave Desert, was built on the bed of a vast dry lake. It has been home to many of aviation's most important and daring feats, from the test flight of the *Bell X-1* (*below*, with crew) to the launch of the U.S. **space shuttles**.

The launch of the space shuttle Columbia on April 12, 1981

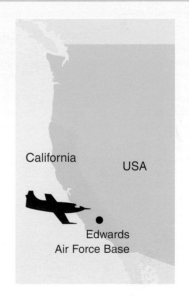

California

USA

Edwards Air Force Base

Muroc Airfield, now renamed Edwards Air Force Base, in California

Ball of Fire

In 1963, Yeager was test-flying the new Lockheed Starfighter at twice the speed of sound when the plane malfunctioned and started to spin out of control. Yeager hit the eject button, but burning debris became caught in his parachute and **pressure suit**. He survived the fall, but needed extensive **skin grafts** before he was back doing what he loved best: flying airplanes!

Chuck Yeager's Starfighter bursts into flames in mid-air. Miraculously, Yeager escaped serious injury.

"I got burned pretty bad on my neck and shoulder and it was very difficult to breathe . . . There is a button on the right, you push it and then you raise your visor. I knew I had to . . . get that visor up to shut the oxygen flow from my kit . . . So I did that. Then I swung a couple times and hit the ground. I couldn't see too much and I was having trouble breathing because there was a lot of smoke and fire. But it worked out . . . I didn't get killed . . ."

Chuck Yeager, on his narrow escape from the blazing Lockheed Starfighter

A 74-year-old Chuck Yeager, photographed on the fiftieth anniversary of his historic flight in the Bell X-1. *After retiring as a test pilot, Yeager joined the Air Force Aerospace Research Pilots' School and trained many of the astronauts in the U.S. Gemini, Mercury, and Apollo space programs.*

Could YOU Be a Test Pilot?

1 What part of being a test pilot would appeal to you the most?

- Being a hero.
- Flying some of the fastest planes in the world.
- Doing something no one has ever done before.
- Being rich and famous.
- The danger.

2 Test your memory by answering these questions:

- At what height was the *Bell X-1* launched before breaking the sound barrier?
- What color was the *Bell X-1* painted?
- What name did Yeager give to all his planes?
- Was the sound barrier first broken in the United States, the UK, or France?

SKY-HIGH ADVENTURE

The Record-Breaking Career of Aviator Steve Fossett

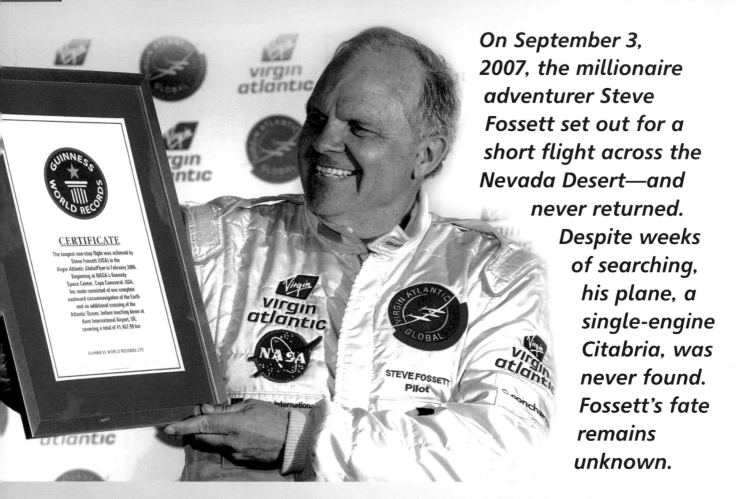

On September 3, 2007, the millionaire adventurer Steve Fossett set out for a short flight across the Nevada Desert—and never returned. Despite weeks of searching, his plane, a single-engine Citabria, was never found. Fossett's fate remains unknown.

Steve Fossett, 1944-2007

Steve Fossett's disappearance was a sad ending to a extraordinary career of record-breaking achievements. Born in Tennessee in 1944, Fossett was rarely out of the news. A world-class aviator, he was also the holder of 116 records in sports ranging from swimming, ballooning, and motor racing to skiing and mountaineering. Few of his exploits attracted greater attention than his 2005 nonstop, solo around-the-world flight in the spectacular *GlobalFlyer*.

> "I do this as a matter of personal satisfaction. To achieve something that is difficult and that stretches my ability to do it."
>
> Steve Fossett on his career as a record-breaking adventurer

GlobalFlyer at a Glance

Built from modern, lightweight materials, *GlobalFlyer* was specially designed to fly nonstop around the world, without refueling. The plane's single jet engine was mounted behind the cockpit on the top of the **fuselage**. The huge quantities of fuel needed for the flight were held in 13 containers along the wings. The landing gear was housed in **booms** on either side of the cockpit.

GlobalFlyer: Vital Statistics

Wing span	114 feet (35 m)
Wing area	400 sq. feet (37 sq m)
Length	44.1 feet (13.44 m)
Height	13 feet (4 m)
Gross weight	22,000 pounds (10 t)
Empty weight	3,700 pounds (1.7 t)
Top speed	286+ miles per hour (460+ km/h)

Engine is mounted behind the cockpit.

Fuel tanks in the wings make up 83% of the plane's weight.

Drag parachutes are stored here to slow the aircraft to landing speed.

N277SF virgin atlantic

6.5–foot (2–m) long pressurized cockpit. Pilot has to sit on cushions to see out during take-off and landing.

Williams **turbo-fan** jet engine uses special fuel with a lower freezing point than standard aviation fuel.

GlobalFlyer *on the tarmac at Salina airport, Kansas. Specially designed and built for Fossett's record-breaking flight, the plane was light but strong enough to carry almost six times its own weight in fuel. However, the wings had no protection against ice or sleet, and the plane was not designed for turbulence.*

Flying High Above the Earth

On the morning of February 8, 2005, Steve Fossett attended his final briefing at Salina airport, Kansas, checked the weather reports, squeezed into the tiny cockpit of *GlobalFlyer,* and taxied down the runway toward takeoff. His attempt on the world's last, great, unbroken aviation record was about to begin.

Flying Blind

A few hours into the flight, Fossett suffered his first setback. Due to a technical fault, the plane's navigation system shut down. For a time, he was flying blind. Fortunately, the system was back in action before he crossed the Atlantic.

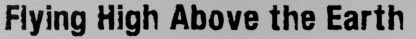

Once in the air, Fossett's plan was to fly at an altitude of at least 8.7 miles (14 km) above the earth's surface—far above the commercial airline traffic and weather systems. With the weight of fuel on board, it would take him more than 14 hours to reach this height.

NORTH AMERICA

Salina, Kansas

SOUTH AMERICA

EUROPE

AFRICA

ASIA

JAPAN

Tokyo

After crossing Japan, Fossett's route would take him south to the Equator where the **jet stream** would help carry the plane across the Pacific.

Worse was to come. On the second day, Fossett discovered that 2,645 pounds (1,200 kg) of fuel had been lost due to a fault in the fuel system. Knowing that a forced landing over the Pacific could be fatal, he considered aborting the flight. Then last-minute talks established that the strong tail winds meant he would need less fuel than he had planned. Fossett pressed on.

On March 3, 2005, at 7:50 P.M., Fossett landed *GlobalFlyer* back at Salina, 67 hours, 1 minute, and 10 seconds after takeoff, having achieved yet another record-breaking flight. He had flown at an average speed of 342 miles per hour (550.7 km/h), making the first solo around-the-world, nonstop, non-refueled flight.

> *"There was no turning back. It was halfway around the world when I found the fuel problem . . . Not only might the flight not have finished, but I might have gotten the plane stuck somewhere."*
>
> Steve Fossett

Could YOU be a record-breaker?

1 Imagine you are flying nonstop around the world in *GlobalFlyer*. What do you think would be the worst part of the flight and why?

   a) The cockpit is very small and hot
   b) Turbulence
   c) Not sleeping

2 What would be the first thing you would say after successfully flying around the world nonstop?

3 After a nonstop, around-the-world flight, what is the first thing you would want to do when you land?

• Go for a long walk
• Have a meal
• Play a video game or watch TV
• Tell all your friends and have a party

Glossary

ace a highly skilled person

adrenaline a chemical released in the body when a person is very excited or scared that helps them to react quickly to danger

boom a special container fitted to the wing of an aircraft

canteen a flask for storing water or other drinks

decorations medals or badges awarded for bravery in wartime

dogfight a fight between military aircraft in the air

Eiffel Tower a famous tower made out of iron in Paris, France

fixed wing a type of aircraft with wings attached to the fuselage

flare a bright light fired from a gun as a distress signal

fuselage the main body of an airplane

high command the top leaders in a military organization

jet stream a current of fast-moving air high in the earth's upper atmosphere

mirage something you think you can see but which is not really there

navigator the person in a plane who plans the journey and guides the pilot

periscope a tube with mirrors, usually used in a submarine to allow the crew to see what is happening on the surface

pressure suit a special suit with an oxygen supply which enables the pilot to breathe when flying at high altitude

radio navigation using radio signals to find out where you are when you are flying a plane or steering a ship

shockwave the force created by a buildup of pressure when a plane flies very fast

skin graft a surgical operation in which healthy skin is moved from one part of the body to another part that has been damaged or injured

sleet a mixture of rain and snow, or partly frozen rain

space shuttle a reusable spacecraft which is used to carry astronauts, rockets, and equipment into space

stunt flyer a pilot who does tricks in the air with his plane to entertain crowds at an air show

superpower a country that dominates the rest of the world, after World War II; the two most powerful countries were the Soviet Union and the United States

supersonic when a plane travels faster than Mach 1 or the speed of sound

telegraph a way of sending messages electronically by wires, usually using Morse Code, a special "alphabet" of short and long signals for sending radio messages

thrust the power a plane builds up in its engine to make sure it can reach a certain speed

time system the time in a particular time zone; for example, in New York the time is three hours ahead of California

triplane a plane that has three sets of wings, one above the other

turbo-fan a type of jet engine often used on airliners that reduces exhaust emissions

vapor cloud a cloud of moisture that forms around a plane when it flies at very high speeds

Index

Web Finder

The Red Baron
www.richthofen.com

Charles Lindbergh
www.charleslindbergh.com

Amelia Earhart
www.lib.purdue.edu/spcol/aearhart/
www.ameliaearhart.com/home.php

Chuck Yeager
www.engineerscouncil.org/Yeager/home.htm

Steve Fossett
www.stevefossett.com/index.html
www.scaled.com/projects/globalflyer.html